D1311289

Everglades National Park

John Hamilton

National Parks

VISIT US AT

WWW.ABDOPUB.COM

Published by ABDO Publishing Company, 4940 Viking Drive, Suite 622, Edina, Minnesota 55435.
Copyright ©2005 by Abdo Consulting Group, Inc. International copyrights reserved in all countries.
No part of this book may be reproduced in any form without written permission from the publisher.
ABDO & Daughters™ is a trademark and logo of ABDO Publishing Company.

Printed in the United States.

Editor: Paul Joseph
Graphic Design: John Hamilton
All photos and illustrations by John Hamilton, except National Park Service, p. 5 (aerial view), p. 10
(aerial view), p. 15 (park map), Seminole Tribe of Florida, p. 14 (Osceola).

Library of Congress Cataloging-in-Publication Data

Hamilton, John, 1959–
    Everglades National Park / John Hamilton.
       p. cm. — (National parks)
    Summary: Discusses the history of this national park, its geological features, trails, wildlife,
dangers in the park, and efforts to preserve it.
    Includes bibliographical references and index.
    ISBN 1-59197-424-0
    1. Everglades National Park (Fla.)—Juvenile literature. [1. Everglades National Park (Fla.)
2. National parks and reserves.] I. Title. II. National parks (ABDO Publishing Company)

F317.E9H36 2005
975.9'39—dc21
                                                        2003041847

Contents

Diversity of Life 5

River of Grass 10

A Balance of Wet and Dry 12

History in the Park 14

Everglades Habitats 16

Alligators 22

Park Highlights 24

Future Challenges 28

Glossary 30

Index 32

Wading birds, such as this great egret, like to hunt for fish in the shallow waters of the Everglades.

The Everglades are home to many large wading birds, including **herons**.

Diversity of Life

When you first cross the boundary into Everglades National Park, you can't help but feel a little disappointed. After traveling all the way to the southern tip of the Florida peninsula, you somehow expect more than what you see—at first. There are no heart-stopping scenic vistas that leap out at you, the kind you'd expect from national parks like the Grand Canyon, or Yellowstone, or Yosemite. Instead, you see an impossibly flat expanse of leafy marshland extending all the way to the horizon, broken only by scattered tangles of mangrove trees and an occasional palm or cypress cluster.

But look closer. Everglades National Park is an International Biosphere Preserve, and for good reason. Few other places in the world have such a rich diversity of plants and wildlife. This fragile ecosystem is home to a stunning variety of animals: panthers, raccoons, black bear, snakes, white-tailed deer, gray fox—the list goes on and on. Underwater habitat is also abundant, ranging from swamps and marshes to estuaries where fresh water meets the sea. Alligators, crocodiles, bottle-nosed dolphins, hammerhead sharks, West Indian manatee, horseshoe crabs, and green sea turtles can all be found in the waters of this single park.

Most well known of all are the Everglades' bird populations, especially the large wading birds like roseate spoonbills, wood storks, ibis, egrets, and great blue herons. Not only do the birds here feed on fish, they also dine on a smorgasbord of insects, just about every kind of creepy, crawly bug you can imagine. During the summer wet season, the clouds of mosquitoes and other insect pests can be unbearable for humans, but the birds here eat like kings.

Everglades National Park is the biggest subtropical wilderness left in the United States. Long ago, almost all the land south of Disneyworld in Orlando, Florida, was a wetland that flooded in the summer, and then partially dried out in the winter months. This climate, with its seasonal cycling of wet and dry, made a rich habitat for wildlife.

Today, the impact of civilization spreads into the Everglades. Where millions of acres of swamp and marshland once existed, now stand a sprawling mass of roads, farms, houses, and shopping malls. A spider-web network of canals and levees diverts the Everglades' precious water resources away from the wetlands. While south Florida's booming population takes the water it needs to drink and irrigate farms, the Everglades suffer.

Everglades National Park was set aside in 1947 to preserve and protect what's left of this fragile, complex ecosystem. There are more than 1.5 million acres (607,029 hectares) of protected land here, making it the third biggest national park in the contiguous United States, after Death Valley and Yellowstone. The Everglades are a refuge for more than 900 plant species and 600 different kinds of animals, including 300 types of birds. The survival of endangered manatee, Florida panthers, and American crocodile also depend on this unique biosphere preserve. But even inside the national park, wetland habitats are disrupted, or are shrinking.

National parks are not islands of protected land. They are affected by what happens outside their borders. Everglades National Park is a good example of this rule. If we hope to protect the strange beauty and diverse wildlife of this place for future generations, we must be mindful of how humans change the environment.

A dragonfly perches on a blade of grass.

Everglades is a term first used in the south Florida area about 1823. In the old English language, "glyde," or "glaed," means a clearing or opening in the forest. There are many small islands in the Everglades that are covered with trees. But the region is mainly a huge river of flatland covered in saw grass. Therefore, if you were to stand in one of the forest islands, you would see all around you a generally unbroken expanse of clearing, or "everglade."

"There are no other Everglades in the world... Nothing anywhere

River of Grass

In 1947, environmentalist Marjory Stoneman Douglas published a book called *The Everglades: River of Grass.* Her words brought attention to the beauty of the Everglades and to the plight of the quickly disappearing ecosystem. She is often called the "mother of the Everglades."

Douglas called the Everglades a river of grass because, contrary to popular belief, the area is not a stagnant swamp. In south-central Florida, summer rains collect in Lake Okeechobee. Water seeps over its banks and slowly flows southward, toward Florida Bay 120 miles (193 km) away. This "river" is over 50 miles (80 km) wide in some places, but it is very shallow, ranging from six inches (15 cm) to about two feet (.6 m) deep.

The water travels slowly, flowing only about 100 feet (30 m) per day. At this rate, it takes three days just to travel the length of a football field, and almost two months to flow one mile (1.6 km)!

As the shallow sheet of water flows steadily southward, it rustles billions of blades of saw grass, which seem to slowly wave as if a giant hand is passing over them. Saw grass gets its name because of the saw-like teeth that line its edges. It can grow to a height of about nine feet (2.7 m). Saw grass can be hazardous to walk through if you don't wear proper clothing. Many animals use thick stands of saw grass as shelter and food.

A shallow sheet of water rustles billions of blades of **saw grass.**

A Balance of Wet and Dry

In south Florida, there are two seasons: wet and dry. The wet season lasts from approximately mid-May to mid-November. Summer rain showers, including hurricanes and tropical storms, dump millions of gallons of water over the area. Water covers most of the Everglades during this time, except for isolated islands of trees. Wildlife and fish scatter all over the park. The wet season can be a difficult time to visit the Everglades, not only because of the rain and hot, muggy air, but also because of the clouds of insects. (In 1893, naturalist Leverett White Brownell wrote that he witnessed an oil lamp extinguished by a swarm of mosquitoes!)

During the sunny, dry season grasslands appear, scattered with pools of brackish water. This is a good time for watching wildlife, especially birds, which gather around the pools of water. Many birds lay their eggs and care for their young during this time.

Over thousands of years, plants and animals in the Everglades have adapted to this wet and dry cycle. When humans construct dikes and levees that alter the flow of water coming into the Everglades, they disrupt the rhythm of life. Sometimes water is let out of dams, flooding the grasslands during the dry season. This destroys many nests and eggs. Other times, when not enough water flows, the pools of water completely dry up, killing the fish and insects that live there, robbing birds and other animals of food. The National Park Service estimates that since the 1930s, 90 percent of the park's wading bird population has vanished.

Many birds, such as this egret (above), gather around the pools of water that are left over during the dry season. Raccoons in the Everglades (below) mainly sleep during the day and come out to feed at night.

History in the Park

Native Americans migrated to the Everglades area at least 11,000 years ago. The "People of the Glades" included the Tequestas and Calusas. Spaniard Juan Ponce de León explored Florida's coastline in the early 1500s, looking for the Fountain of Youth. He opened Florida to Spanish rule. After 250 years of slave raids and diseases, the People of the Glades were nearly wiped out.

By the early 1800s, Florida was controlled by the United States. Thousands of Seminole Indians from north Florida had moved into the Everglades area. Conflict with white settlers led to three wars. By the mid-1800s, most of the Seminoles had been moved west of the Mississippi River by the U.S. government. Today, many Seminoles live on reservations on the fringes of Everglades National Park.

Seminole leader Osceola.

Developers flocked to the south Florida area in the early 1900s. The Everglades were thought of as a giant, useless swamp that needed to be drained and controlled. Roads and towns were built, dikes and levees tamed the waterways, and hunters slaughtered huge numbers of wading birds for their colorful plumes.

Thanks to the efforts of conservationists like Ernest F. Coe and Marjory Stoneman Douglas, the public realized that the Everglades would quickly disappear unless a portion of it was set aside. On December 6, 1947, President Harry S. Truman dedicated Everglades National Park, setting aside this one-of-a-kind wilderness for future generations to enjoy.

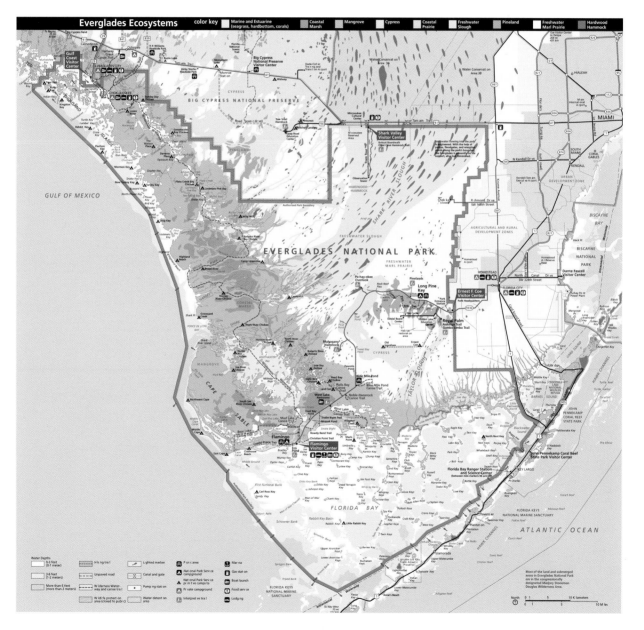

Everglades Habitats

Everglades National Park boasts several distinct ecosystems, each of which has its own population of unique plants and animals. Starting at the south end of the park, between the Florida Keys and the southern tip of Florida, is the *marine/estuary* environment of Florida Bay. An estuary is where fresh water flows into the salty water of an ocean. Some of the Everglades' marine animals include bottle-nosed dolphins, hammerhead sharks, and stingrays. Shrimp, spiny lobster, and conch inhabit the shallow, seagrass-covered bottom, which is made of hard limestone. Coral and sponges also live here.

Coastal prairie is found between the tidal mud flats of Florida Bay and dry land. Conditions can be harsh here when the land is battered by heavy winds and hurricane flooding. Tough plants like coconut palms and red mangrove grow here, as well as saw grass. Green sea turtles, frogs, and marsh rabbits can be found in coastal prairie areas.

Farther inland are the *mangrove forests*. Mangrove trees are easily spotted because their roots look like stilts. They can grow in salt water, so they do well in tidal estuaries. Their above-ground roots help them breathe when their underground roots get covered with water. They are very strong, which helps them to survive during hurricanes and tropical storms. The roots also provide a natural nursery for shrimp and fish. White-tail deer and roseate spoonbills like to make their home in mangrove forests. Many other kinds of birds also gather and nest in mangrove trees during the dry season.

The interior of a hardwood hammock (above) is densely packed with foliage, offering protection for many kinds of animals, such as raccoons and fox. Alligators (below) make their home in the Everglades' freshwater habitats.

A *freshwater slough* (pronounced "sloo") is the deepest and fastest-flowing part of the Everglades' broad marshy river. Scattered throughout the slough are shallow rises of limestone, which create small tree-covered islands called hammocks. Hardwoods such as mahogany, oak, and gumbo-limbo trees are often found growing on hammocks. These sheltered islands are frequently home to gray fox, raccoon, and other small animals. Snakes like to inhabit the outer edges of hammocks, and wood ducks, snapping turtles, and spotted gar can be found swimming nearby. The two main freshwater sloughs in the Everglades are the Shark River Slough, which is often called the "river of grass," and the Taylor Slough, which is a narrower, eastern branch of the main river.

Cypress domes are thick stands of bald cypress that have grown in water-filled holes. Trees in the middle grow taller because the soil at the center of the hole is deeper. They are called bald cypress because they lose their needles every fall, unlike most other conifer trees.

Pinelands grow in the driest part of the Everglades, on top of limestone ridges that jut up a few feet above the surrounding landscape. Pine somehow manages to grow in any crack or crevice where soil collects in the bedrock. The Everglades' pinelands are very diverse in plants and wildlife, including saw palmettos and over 200 other kinds of tropical plants. Many kinds of snakes live here, as well as a variety of birds, including barred owl.

Scattered throughout the Everglades' freshwater slough habitat are tree-covered islands called hammocks, which shelter many kinds of birds and animals.

An endangered female snail kite (above) is perched at a clearing near a cypress dome.
These birds eat apple snails, which they snatch out of the water with their sharp talons.
Pinelands (below) grow in the driest part of the Everglades.

A great egret (above) hunts for food on a foggy morning. Large wading bird populations in the park have steadily declined as human development has affected water supplies in the park. A grasshopper (below) takes shelter in a hardwood hammock.

Park visitors admire the view of Florida Bay (above) from the beach at Flamingo, at the southern tip of Everglades National Park. A hardwood hammock supports dense vegetation (below) that is used by many birds and animals to nest or hide.

Alligators

The "king of the Everglades" is the American alligator. This large reptile can be found all over the park. During the dry season, which lasts from about mid November to mid May, they are easiest to spot in standing pools of water that are called gator holes. Alligators dig out these pockets in the ground, which then become important gathering places for fish, turtles, and wading birds during the drier months. Many of these creatures would not survive the dry season without gator holes.

Young alligators are about 10 inches (25 cm) long, but when they become adults, they can grow to be monsters measuring 12 feet long (3.7 m) and weighing 600 pounds (272 kg). The biggest alligator ever found in the Everglades measured 17 feet, 5 inches (5.3 m), about the length of three adult humans laid end to end.

Although alligators may seem docile and lazy, especially when basking in the sun, they can hit speeds up to 30 miles per hour (38 kph) for short distances. It's never a good idea to get too close to an alligator if you find one basking on the blacktop of an Everglades footpath, although attacks on humans are very rare.

Hunted almost to extinction for their meat and hide, alligators in recent years have made a comeback. Their biggest threats today in the Everglades are releases of water into the ecosystem by dams and levees upstream. The rising water often destroys alligator nests.

American crocodiles are also found in the Everglades. They are related to the alligator, but have a narrower snout and are olive brown in color. They also can live in salty estuary water. They are an endangered species; only a few hundred are left in the wild. The Everglades is the only place in the world where alligators and crocodiles live side by side.

The American alligator (above) is often called "king of the Everglades." They are easiest to spot during the dry season, when they rest in standing pools of water called gator holes. They dig these holes with their powerful tails, snouts, and feet (below).

Park Highlights

Although Everglades National Park is one of the biggest parks in the country, there is only one main road that takes visitors through the heart of the area. To see more of the park, you have to go by boat. Guided tours on large boats are available, but many people like to explore by canoe. The Wilderness Waterway is a 99-mile (159-km) canoe route that takes paddlers through the estuary fringe on the west side of the park, from Everglades City in the north all the way to Florida Bay in the south.

For visitors touring by car, the main road starts at the park's east entrance near Homestead, Florida, just southwest of Miami. The Ernest F. Coe Visitor Center is a good place to begin. Named after the famed naturalist who did so much to preserve the Everglades, the center has a lot of information about the park, and also educates visitors about the continuing threats to this watery wilderness.

The rest of the 38-mile (61-km) drive takes you through a good sampling of the Everglades ecosystems, all the way south to the tiny town of Flamingo, on the shores of Florida Bay.

The drive is especially beautiful early in the morning or at dusk, when more birds and animals appear. The flat landscape rolls past, with a seemingly endless expanse of saw grass dotted with small islands of trees. There are many places to stop and absorb the scenery. Muted greens, browns, and oranges greet the eyes. The atmosphere here is humid and fragrant. The smell of dense vegetation, brackish water, and wildflowers fills the air. Overhead, the tropical Florida sun beats down. In the wet season, tall white clouds pile up on the horizon, preparing to drop sheets of summer rain.

A great egret (above) sits perched on a tree branch near the Pa-hay-okee Overlook. Pa-hay-okee is a Native American name for the Everglades that means "grassy waters." Gulls rest near a tour boat at the Flamingo marina (below).

There are several places where the National Park Service has built walkways or maintained trails through this wet landscape. The Anhinga Trail, the Gumbo Limbo Trail, or the Pineland Trail are good spots to take early-morning walks. If you stand quiet, you can hear Everglades activity all around you: the sound of water trickling past, insects droning, snowy egrets taking flight, the eerie resonance of alligators calling to one another, or a heron snapping its head into shallow water to spear a fish with its beak.

At the end of the drive is Flamingo, on the shores of Florida Bay. Here you can camp, take boat tours, or hike along the waterfront. Raccoons, roseate spoonbills, and black bear are often spotted here. In the marina, you can sometimes see manatees bobbing in the water.

There are two other areas of the Everglades that are often visited. The Shark Valley Visitor Center is on the northeastern border of the park. The main attraction is a 15-mile (24-km) loop road that you can hike or bicycle or, during the summer, take a 2-hour narrated tram ride. You can see a great deal of wildlife from the trail, especially alligators, turtles, and wading birds. Sometimes the rare Florida panther is spotted in this area. At the end of the trail is an elevated 65-foot (19.8-m) tower that gives a bird's-eye view of the Everglades.

Everglades City is a small town in the northwestern corner of the park. There are regularly scheduled narrated boat tours that leave from here, taking you through the Ten Thousand Islands part of the Gulf of Mexico. The waters around these mangrove islands hold many protected species, including bottle-nosed dolphins and manatees. Pelicans and cormorants are common birds in the area.

The marina at the Gulf Coast Visitor Center in Everglades City.

Raised walkways, like this one at Pa-hay-okee Overlook (above), let visitors see sections of the park that would be normally inaccessible because of dense, swampy underbrush. The marina at Flamingo has boats available for backcountry day trips (below).

Future Challenges

The biggest threat to the Everglades today is the altered waterflow to the park caused by human development. This disruption has caused a drastic decline in wildlife in and around the park, especially in bird populations.

Another serious problem involves toxic chemicals, especially mercury, that find their way into the Everglades' ecosystem. Many farmers on land neighboring the park spray their crops with pesticides and fertilizers, which mix with the water flowing into the park. This pollution is slowly killing the wildlife in the Everglades.

Another problem is the invasion of non-native plants and animals that crowd out the natural inhabitants. Plants such as melaleuca trees, imported from Australia, grow quickly and dry out the soil. Pet owners who can no longer care for their animals sometimes release exotic reptiles such as boa constrictors into the Everglades. They thrive in the subtropical climate and kill off native wildlife.

The Comprehensive Everglades Restoration Plan is a multi-year effort by state and federal government agencies, as well as independent scientists and members of the Seminole and Miccosukee Indian tribes, to partially restore the wetlands. The plan is to redirect more water to Lake Okeechobee and remove some dikes and levees to restore the natural water flow, plus build artificial marshes around the Everglades to buffer the effects of cities and farms. Air pollution regulations are also being tightened to limit the amount of mercury that settles into the park.

As the human population in south Florida continues to grow, there will be more pressure on the Everglades. Hopefully, an educated public will help create a balance between the demands of people and the needs of this unique, fragile ecosystem.

Sunrise at the east entrance to Everglades National Park.

Glossary

ECOSYSTEM

A biological community of animals, plants, and bacteria, all of whom live together in the same physical or chemical environment.

FEDERAL LANDS

Much of America's land, especially in the western part of the country, is maintained by the United States federal government. These are public lands owned by all U.S. citizens. There are many kinds of federal lands. National parks, like the Everglades, are federal lands that are set aside so that they can be preserved. Other federal lands, such as national forests or national grasslands, are used in many different ways, including logging, ranching, and mining. Much of the land surrounding the Everglades is maintained by the government, including several national preserves and wildlife refuges.

FOREST SERVICE

The United States Department of Agriculture (USDA) Forest Service was started in 1905 to manage public lands in national forests and grasslands. The Forest Service today oversees an area of 191 million acres (77.3 million hectares), which is an amount of land about the same size as Texas. In addition to protecting and managing America's public lands, the Forest Service also conducts forestry research and helps many state government and private forestry programs.

GEOLOGICAL SURVEY

The United States Geological Survey was created in 1879. It is an independent science agency that is part of the Department of the Interior. It researches and collects facts about the land of the United States, giving us a better understanding of our natural resources.

Levee

A levee is a big embankment, often made of dirt, that is constructed next to a river or lake to keep high water from flooding neighboring land. Networks of levees near Everglades National Park have interrupted the natural flow of water into the park, severely affecting plants and wildlife.

Subtropical Zone

Subtropical climate zones, including south Florida, border true tropical zones. They aren't quite as hot and humid, but still have many of the same kinds of plants and animals, like palm trees and alligators, that one would expect to find in the tropics.

Wetland

An area of land that usually has standing water for most of the year, like swamps or marshes. Many wetlands, like the Everglades, have been set aside as preserves for wildlife. Many kinds of birds and animals depend on this habitat for nesting, food, and shelter.

A snowy egret in flight over the Everglades.

Index

A

Anhinga Trail 26
Australia 28

B

Brownell, Leverett
   White 12

C

Calusa 14
Coe, Ernest F. 14,
   24
Comprehensive
   Everglades
   Restoration Plan
   28

D

de León, Juan
   Ponce 14
Death Valley
   National Park 6
Disneyworld 6
Douglas, Marjory
   Stoneman 10,
   14

E

Ernest F. Coe
   Visitor Center
   24
Everglades City,
   FL 25, 26
*Everglades: River of
   Grass, The* 10

F

Flamingo, FL 24,
   26
Florida 5, 6, 7, 10,
   12, 14, 16, 24,
   26, 28
Florida Bay 10,
   16, 24, 26
Florida Keys 16
Fountain of Youth
   14

G

Grand Canyon
   National Park 5
Gulf of Mexico
   26
Gumbo Limbo
   Trail 26

H

Homestead, FL
   24

I

International
   Biosphere
   Preserve 5

L

Lake Okeechobee
   10, 28

M

Miami, FL 24

Miccosukee 28
Mississippi River
   14

N

National Park
   Service 12, 26

O

Orlando, FL 6

P

People of the
   Glades 14
Pineland Trail 26

S

Seminole 14, 28
Shark River
   Slough 18
Shark Valley
   Visitor Center
   26

T

Taylor Slough 18
Ten Thousand
   Islands 26
Tequesta 14
Truman, Harry S.
   14

U

United States 6,
   14

W

Wilderness
   Waterway 24

Y

Yellowstone
   National Park
   5, 6
Yosemite National
   Park 5